LIVING LEGENDS OF SPORTS

RUSSELL WESTBROOK

TRIPLE-DOUBLE SUPERSTAR

RYAN NAGELHOUT

Britannica Educational Publishing

IN ASSOCIATION WITH

ROSEN EDUCATIONAL SERVICES

Published in 2019 by Britannica Educational Publishing (a trademark of Encyclopædia Britannica, Inc.) in association with The Rosen Publishing Group, Inc.
29 East 21st Street, New York, NY 10010

Distributed exclusively by Rosen Publishing.
To see additional Britannica Educational Publishing titles, go to rosenpublishing.com.

First Edition

Britannica Educational Publishing
J.E. Luebering: Executive Director, Core Editorial
Andrea R. Field: Managing Editor, Compton's by Britannica

Rosen Publishing
Kathy Kuhtz Campbell: Senior Editor
Nelson Sá: Art Director
Nicole Russo-Duca: Series Designer and Book Layout
Cindy Reiman: Photography Manager
Sherri Jackson: Photo Researcher

Library of Congress Cataloging-in-Publication Data

Names: Nagelhout, Ryan.
Title: Russell Westbrook : triple-double superstar / Ryan Nagelhout.
Description: New York : Britannica Educational Publishing, in Association with Rosen Educational Services, 2019 | Series: Living legend of sports | Includes bibliographical references and index. | Audience: Grades 5-8.
Identifiers: LCCN 2017053339| ISBN 9781538302231 (library bound) | ISBN 9781538302248 (pbk.)
Subjects: LCSH: Westbrook, Russell, 1988—Juvenile literature. | Basketball players—United States—Biography—Juvenile literature.
Classification: LCC GV884.W44 N34 2019 | DDC 796.323092 [B] –dc23
LC record available at https://lccn.loc.gov/2017053339

Manufactured in the United States of America

Photo credits: Cover, pp. 1, 39 J Pat Carter/Getty Images; cover and interior pages background © iStockphoto.com/block37; p. 5 Misael Montano/LatinContent WO/Getty Images; pp. 7, 9 Lilly Lawrence/Getty Images; p. 10 Jim McIsaac/Getty Images; p. 12 Ken Hively/Los Angeles Times/Getty Images; p. 13 Ron Jenkins/Fort Worth Star-Telegram/Tribune News Service/Getty Images; p. 15 Jeff Gross/Getty Images; pp. 16-17 Sporting News Archive/Getty Images; pp. 18, 21, 24, 37 © AP Images; p. 19 MCT/Tribune News Service/Getty Images; p. 25 Dilip Vishwanat/Getty Images; pp. 26-27, 28-29 Ronald Martinez/Getty Images; pp. 30, 33 Icon Sports Wire/Getty Images; p. 35 Paul Zimmerman/WireImage/Getty Images; p. 36 Lachlan Cunningham/Getty Images.

CONTENTS

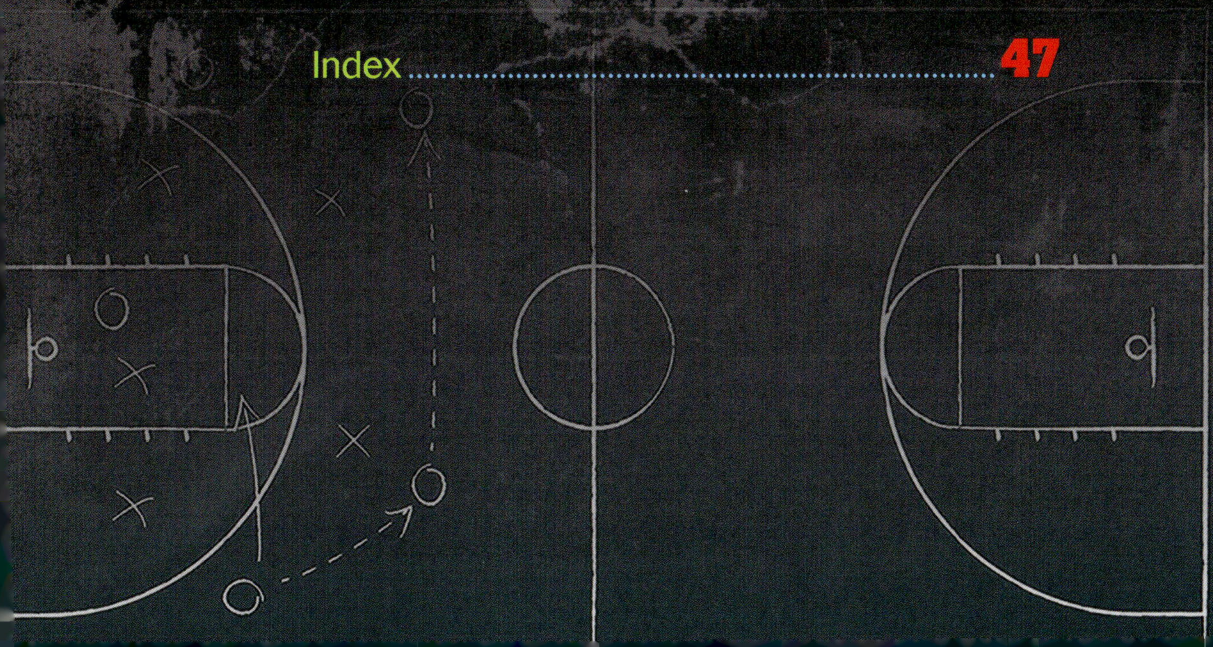

INTRO-DUCTION

Russell Westbrook and Kevin Durant turned the Oklahoma City Thunder into a powerhouse in the Western Conference of the National Basketball Association (NBA). The franchise, which moved from Seattle to Oklahoma City shortly after Durant and Westbrook joined the team in 2008, quickly took root in its new home.

Together, Westbrook and Durant helped the Thunder reach the playoffs six times, including a trip to the NBA Finals in 2012. But after the Thunder blew a 3–1 lead to the Golden State Warriors in the 2016 Western Conference Finals, Durant faced free agency and a chance for a fresh start.

Rather than stay in Oklahoma City with his friend, he joined the team that beat them: the Golden State Warriors. It was a landscape-altering decision for Durant and one that shocked Oklahoma City. It also shocked Westbrook, who would soon face his own free agency decision in 2018.

Many thought that Westbrook's best chance of something great had just walked out the door. The two had been both teammates and friends. When Durant won league Most Valuable Player (MVP) honors in May 2014, he expressed his gratitude to Russ at length with a heartfelt speech in which he famously thanked just about everyone in his life:

> *I know you guys think I forgot Russ. But I could speak all night about Russell. An emotional guy who will run through a wall for me. I don't take it for granted … A lot of people put unfair criticism on you as a player and I'm the first to have your back, man, through it all. Just stay the person you are.*

Russell Westbrook has become a mainstay in the Oklahoma City community through his play on the court and his charity outside of sports.

Everybody loves you here … You make me better … You set the tone … You're an MVP-caliber player. It's a blessing to play with you, man.

When Durant left Westbrook behind, though, their friendship was shattered. And it seemed clear that the Thunder would struggle. Many people thought that Westbrook would not be able to carry the Thunder on his own.

But those skeptics knew little about Russell Westbrook. Without Durant, the Thunder superstar transformed into one of the greatest scoring threats in the league. After Durant left, what followed was one of the most legendary individual seasons in NBA history.

Westbrook has changed into a force of nature in the NBA. But perhaps more important, he has become one of basketball's most unique stars. From his sense of style to his work ethic on and off the court, Westbrook has proven his star power and hustle countless times in his NBA career. Furthermore, he has proven his commitment to the people around him, including those in Oklahoma City.

Westbrook has gone above and beyond any expectations he had growing up in Long Beach, California. Durant was right about one thing: the point guard was—and is—MVP-caliber.

CHAPTER ONE

Why Not Russ?

Russell Westbrook III was born on November 12, 1988, in Long Beach, California. His parents—Russell Westbrook Jr. and Shannon Horton—raised him in Hawthorne, California. The couple also had another son, Russell's younger brother, Raynard.

Westbrook poses with members of his family: (*left to right*) his wife, Nina; his brother, Raynard; and his parents, Shannon and Russell Jr.

QUICK FACT

When Russ was little, his dad had him shoot 500 shots a day in the gym.

Russell Westbrook Jr. worked at a bread factory while his wife worked at a public school cafeteria in Los Angeles. The Westbrooks' son loved school and basketball. His favorite subject in school was math. And he was very smart! But basketball soon became an obsession for Russ.

When Russ was seven, he started shadowing his father at Ross Snyder Park, a recreation center in Los Angeles. His favorite pro player was Earvin "Magic" Johnson, who played for the Los Angeles Lakers.

Russ grew quickly, just like much of his family. Though his father is just 5 feet 8 inches tall, Westbrook's grandfather was 6 feet 1 inch tall, and his grandfather's sister is 6 feet 2. But he never grew to become a 7-footer like some who dominate the NBA. He eventually topped out at 6 feet 3.

Learning and Practice

Russ was far from a natural basketball talent right away. Getting into the NBA takes countless hours of training and working out, both on and off the court. Russ would even do pull-ups at home on a bar his parents put up on their patio.

Reggie Hamilton, Russ's first basketball coach, knew early on how determined he was. They first met when Russ was nine. Hamilton coached a team called the LA Elite that was based at Jesse Owens Park gym. He said that Russ was always very focused, even as a child.

Westbrook's dad said he knew his son was going to be something special when he insisted on spending part of Thanksgiving Day during his freshman year of high school practicing his shot.

"He said 'Dad, I know it's Thanksgiving. But I want to shoot. Let's go shoot,'" Russ's father told Darnell Mayberry of the *Oklahoman* in 2011.

All that practice was for a reason, though. Russ "couldn't shoot a lick" according to Hamilton. But he was very emotional and driven,

Westbrook (*far left*) helps out at his Why Not? Foundation's basketball camp at Jesse Owens Park in Los Angeles in 2017. He inspires young basketball players much as his first coach, Reggie Hamilton, inspired him.

which came through on the court. "He was very competitive from a real young age," Hamilton told the *Oklahoman*. "He did not like to lose. And he definitely always played hard. So that was a good, positive thing right off the bat."

An Early Loss

QUICK FACT

Russ wore a size 14 shoe when he was just 15 years old!

Growing up, Russ played basketball with his best friend, Khelcey Barrs III. Barrs was a great player in high school, starting for Leuzinger High School in Lawndale, California, as a freshman.

"Khelcey and I both definitely wanted to go to UCLA," Russ later told ESPN. "Go there together and then go to the NBA."

In May 2004, their high school coach took Russ and Khelcey to Los Angeles Southwest College to play pickup basketball against some high

The KB3 wristband Westbrook wears during games is a tribute to a lost friend. His other wristband bears his personal motto, "Why not?"

school and college athletes. The two were just 10th graders, but Khelcey was playing well according to his friend.

"I remember Khelcey was playing maybe the best I'd seen him play in a long time," Russ told ESPN.

But soon after Russ left, his best friend collapsed and died. Doctors found out after Khelcey's death that he had an enlarged heart. He was only 16. Khelcey's death stunned Russ, who would go across the street to do his friend's chores for his family after he died.

To this day, Russell Westbrook wears a wristband with "KB3" on it. The tribute has also appeared on his shoes. Russ told ESPN that remembering his friend makes him play better. "I want people to know that Khelcey could have been the best player in the country," he said. "Khelcey's always going to be a part of my life."

Another wristband Russ wears has the saying "Why not?" on it. It is another major lesson he learned when he was young, and it has become a personal motto for the point guard. "A few of my friends came up with it in high school and it was something that got me far in life and obviously to this point not just in basketball just in life," Russ said in a 2017 interview. "Anytime somebody would tell you that you couldn't do something, I always told myself 'Why not? I can be the best. Why not?'"

Only One Friend

Russ was not always the great basketball player that he is today, though he did play hard. He could not dunk as a junior, and he often struggled with shooting. But he was determined.

"I have one friend," he used to say before games, according to Lee Jenkins of *Sports Illustrated*, "and that's this ball."

Russ's passion for the game is usually a great asset—but not always. "I'm so emotional and I want to win so badly that it can backfire," he told Jenkins. "Controlling it, using it to my advantage, has been the challenge."

Coaches who saw him play at Leuzinger described Russ as immature and undersized and inconsistent. He averaged 25.1 points, 8.7 rebounds, and 2.3 assists per game during his senior season. But

Westbrook had a growth spurt before his senior year of high school, gaining five inches in height.

Westbrook is all smiles during a practice. Many scouts were not sure he could play at the highest level of college basketball, but he would make a mark at UCLA.

he only started in his junior and senior years, unlike many high school hoops phenoms. "I just knew that I had to get better each and every year," Russ told Darnell Mayberry. "That's what I tried to do."

He was getting better, but it would take a long time for people to notice just how good he could be.

QUICK FACT

Westbrook cannot grow a beard. He claims that he has never had to shave!

CHAPTER TWO

UCLA to OKC

College basketball seemed to be in Russell Westbrook's future. But the school he and Khelcey wanted to attend—the University of California at Los Angeles (UCLA)—was not a sure thing. For most of his high school career, Westbrook was recruited heavily only by San Diego. In 2004, Westbrook played in an Amateur Athletic Union (AAU) tournament at UCLA. Westbrook was still not seeing many scholarship offers, but he impressed the organizer of the tournament enough that he told coaches at the school they should give him a look.

The UCLA coaches looked into the kid and liked what they saw. But Westbrook had to wait, as UCLA could not offer him a scholarship until late in his senior year. Although many high school hoops prospects had decided their futures months or even years earlier, Westbrook did not sign a letter of intent to the school until February of his senior year.

Westbrook got to go to his dream school to play basketball, but expectations were not very high for him as a freshman. A spot on the team opened up when star Jordan Farmar left for the NBA. But Westbrook would not take his spot in the starting lineup as a freshman.

In fact, many experts thought he was not good enough to play at a school like UCLA and against the level of competition he would see in the Pacific-10 (Pac-10) Conference. Westbrook was ranked as the 151st college prospect in the country when he came to UCLA, and it would take some time for him to prove his doubters wrong.

Westbrook did not see much playing time early in his UCLA career. He became a starter only in his sophomore year.

SPALDING
FINAL FOUR
NIAGARA
NORTH TEXAS
UCLA
3
FLORIDA
42
FLORIDA

Westbrook (*center*) and the Bruins try to score against the Florida Gators in a Final Four matchup during the 2007 NCAA Tournament. The Bruins lost the game by a score of 76–66.

To the Final Four

Westbrook played just two seasons at UCLA, but he and the Bruins found success while he was on the team. He came off the bench as a freshman but played in all 36 games for the Bruins, averaging 3.4 points, 0.8 rebounds, and 0.7 assists per game. He made an impact with his speed and work ethic on the court. Though he never played more than eight minutes in a game of the National Collegiate Athletic Association (NCAA) Tournament, he scored in each game. And UCLA made it to the Final Four, losing to Florida in a national semifinal game on March 31, 2007.

As a sophomore in the 2007–08 season, Westbrook had a much bigger role on the team. And freshman Kevin Love, a forward, was a key addition to the program. UCLA won the Pac-10 Tournament and returned to the Final Four, losing this time to Memphis in a national semifinal game.

Westbrook and Kevin Love (*right*) became close friends on the UCLA men's basketball team.

Love and Westbrook became fast friends and were roommates on the road. But Westbrook gave Love a hard time when they first met. In an article in the *Players' Tribune* in 2016, Love said that Westbrook poked fun at his lack of style.

Love, a future NBA star himself, said they got along great at UCLA, except when it came to the temperature of their dormitory room. Love said that Westbrook wanted it very warm—74 degrees Fahrenheit—while Love wanted it much cooler.

Love and Westbrook both left UCLA after the 2007–08 season, deciding to enter the NBA Draft. The two went to the NBA Draft Combine, where they were among more than 70 players trying to impress NBA scouts.

Westbrook blocks a shot by Derrick Rose of the Memphis Tigers in an NCAA national semifinal game in 2008. UCLA lost the game and was eliminated from the tournament. Westbrook had raised his profile in his sophomore season, however, and would soon become a first-round NBA draft pick.

But was Westbrook a top prospect? His statistics had improved in his sophomore season, when he averaged 12.7 points, 3.9 rebounds, and 4.3 assists per game. But his overall college numbers were not very impressive. He had started just 35 of 75 games, with averages of 8.3 points, 2.4 rebounds, and 2.5 assists per game.

QUICK FACT

At the 2008 NBA Draft Combine, Westbrook was 6 feet 3.5 inches tall and weighed 192 pounds. He was measured to have a wingspan of 6 feet 7.75 inches and a vertical leap of 36.5 inches.

Making an Impression

In a pre-draft workout with the Seattle SuperSonics, Westbrook tried to dunk so hard that he would break the rim. He failed, but the team certainly took notice. "His wrists," Sonics trainer Rob McClanaghan told Lee Jenkins, "were red afterward."

There was talk that Westbrook could go in the first round of the draft, maybe even before his friend Kevin Love. The Sonics were very interested in him. Though he was a bit reckless, they thought they could teach him how to be a point guard in the NBA. Westbrook certainly tried his best to impress them.

QUICK FACT

Kevin Love was drafted by the Memphis Grizzlies but was traded right away to the Minnesota Timberwolves.

On June 26, 2008, the Sonics selected Westbrook with the fourth pick in the NBA Draft. There were trade rumors surrounding the pick, but the Sonics stayed with him.

Many in the NBA community were surprised that Westbrook went before Love. Many major analysts said the Sonics would regret their pick. Sam Presti, the general manager of the Sonics, was not bothered by

NBA Commissioner David Stern (*left*) congratulates Westbrook after the Seattle SuperSonics selected him with the fourth pick of the 2008 NBA Draft.

the criticism. He said that Westbrook was one of the best defensive players in the draft and noted his drive on the court.

"His competitors have tremendous respect for him," Presti told Percy Allen of the *Seattle Times* after the draft. "And his teammates have tremendous respect for him. That kind of character and defensive mentality are what we're attracted to."

Westbrook was not concerned about what anyone was saying about him, either. He was thrilled that the team believed in him. The Sonics thought he was ready for the NBA, and Westbrook was eager to prove them right. But they would change names before he got the chance to play in a Sonics uniform.

CHAPTER THREE

Sonic to Thunder

In 2006, two years before Westbrook was drafted, an Oklahoma businessman named Clay Bennett led a group of investors in a bid to buy the Seattle SuperSonics. Bennett's group bought the team for $350 million and began asking for a new arena in Seattle. Much of the next two years was full of controversy in Washington State. The city of Seattle sued the Sonics ownership group to keep the team in the city. Bennett demanded a new arena for the team and insisted that taxpayers fund most of the project.

The city refused, however, and so in 2008 the Seattle SuperSonics were moved to Oklahoma City. The team was renamed the Thunder, and Westbrook and former Sonics star Kevin Durant led a new-look franchise in Oklahoma.

Westbrook's rookie year in Oklahoma City, 2008–09, was not very successful. The Thunder went 23–59. He played in all 82 games, though, starting at guard in 65 games. Westbrook averaged 15.3 points, 5.3 assists, and 4.9 rebounds per game as a rookie. He was named to the NBA's All-Rookie First Team.

QUICK FACT

Westbrook signed his rookie contract on July 4, 2008, for about $6 million over two seasons.

Westbrook *(far right)* and Kevin Durant (*second from right*) try to gain control of the ball in a 2009 game against Portland.

His second year with the Thunder (2009–10) saw improvements in his numbers (16.1 points, 8.0 assists, 4.9 rebounds per game) and in Oklahoma City's play. The Thunder finished the regular season with a record of 50–32 and made the playoffs. Westbrook played well in the postseason, averaging 20.5 points, 6.0 rebounds, and 6.0 assists per game. The Thunder, however, lost to the Los Angeles Lakers in the first round.

Westbrook grabs a rebound against the Los Angeles Lakers during Game Six of the Thunder's first-round playoff series in 2010. The Thunder lost the game by a point and were eliminated from the playoffs.

An NBA All-Star

In the 2010–11 season, the Thunder went to the Western Conference Finals and Westbrook made his first NBA All-Star Game. He averaged 21.9 points per game, a big jump from the previous year. In 2011–12, the Thunder went to the NBA Finals. The regular season was cut short by a lockout, but Westbrook, Durant, and James Harden led the team to a 47–19 record and a Finals matchup against the Miami Heat. In a Game 4 loss, Westbrook scored a playoff career-high 43 points, but Oklahoma City lost the series in five games.

Harden was traded to the Houston Rockets after the 2011–12 season. Westbrook and Durant became a true 1–2 punch for the Thunder, and both would make the All-Star Game in the coming seasons. Westbrook averaged 23.2 points, 7.4 assists, 5.2 rebounds, and 1.8 steals per game in the 2012–13 season,

QUICK FACT

Westbrook won a gold medal in the 2012 London Olympic Games as a member of Team USA.

Westbrook tries to steal the ball from LeBron James of the Miami Heat in Game Five of the 2012 NBA Finals.

and the Thunder were the top seed in the NBA's Western Conference.

But in Game 2 of their opening playoff series against the Houston Rockets, Westbrook hurt his right knee when he collided with Patrick Beverley. Though Westbrook finished the game, he had torn his right meniscus and needed surgery that kept him out of the rest of the playoffs. Without Westbrook, the Thunder went on to lose to the Memphis Grizzlies in the next round.

The injury forced Westbrook to miss the first two games of the 2013–14 season, and he needed surgery on his right knee again later in the season. But when he was healthy, he shined. He averaged 21.8 points, 6.9 assists, and 5.7 rebounds per game in just 46 regular-season

QUICK FACT

Westbrook loves the people who work for the Oklahoma City Thunder. He even goes to some of their family events!

Westbrook tries to score against the San Antonio Spurs in Game Six of the 2014 Western Conference Finals. The Thunder lost the game by a score of 112–107.

Westbrook scores against the Milwaukee Bucks on December 29, 2015. He and Kevin Durant led the Thunder to a 131–123 win. Westbrook scored 27 points and had seven assists and seven rebounds in the game.

games. Once again, though, postseason success eluded the Thunder. Though Westbrook averaged 26.7 points per game in the playoffs, Oklahoma City lost in the Western Conference Finals to the San Antonio Spurs, who went on to win the NBA title.

The Maniac

According to Westbrook's teammates, he becomes a changed person before games. He listens to lots of different music to get pumped up for the game.

"He doesn't talk," former teammate Anthony Morrow told Lee Jenkins. "He doesn't blink. He turns into Maniac Russ."

Westbrook's constant drive is a source of pride for him and of admiration from others around the league. Although some players might not give their all every night because they're tired or saving energy for later, Westbrook says he does not have an off switch.

"There are many times throughout a season that you may not feel like playing," he told Jenkins. "You may not want to play on this night, or against this team. But I don't feel that way. This is one of the best jobs in the world, and you never know how long you'll be able to do it—how long you'll be able to run like this and jump like this. So I go for it. I go for it every time. It may look angry, but it's the only way I know."

Durant sat out much of the 2014–15 season with foot and ankle injuries. With Durant on the bench, Westbrook took over the Thunder. He led the league in scoring, averaging 28.1 points, 8.6 assists, and 7.3 rebounds per game. The Thunder missed the playoffs for the first time since 2008–09, but Westbrook's dominance was a sign of things to come.

Westbrook was asked if he was playing his best, and he said he might be at his peak at the moment before reconsidering. "I don't know if it's the height," he told Jenkins, "or the beginning."

He had no idea how right he was.

CHAPTER FOUR

Going Solo

The Thunder roared back to the playoffs in the 2015–16 season. Behind the dominant play of Westbrook and Durant, the team reached the Western Conference Finals for a matchup against the Golden State Warriors. Oklahoma City won the first game, 108–102. The Warriors pushed back in Game 2, winning 118–91. In Game 3, the Thunder posted an impressive 133–105 win. Westbrook scored 36 points in the fourth game, which the Thunder won 118–94. But the Warriors fought back to win the next three games and reach the NBA Finals. It was a devastating defeat for the Thunder that left the team wanting more.

But if the Thunder were going to avenge the loss, they would have to do it without Durant. Before the 2016–17 season began, Durant left the Thunder to join the Warriors, leaving Westbrook as the only star in Oklahoma City. It was a big test for Westbrook, and he passed with flying colors. He would go on to have one of the greatest individual seasons in NBA history.

The Thunder went 47–35 in the regular season, making the playoffs as the sixth seed in the Western Conference. They lost in the first round of the playoffs to the Houston Rockets. But once again, Westbrook was outstanding. In fact, he became a triple-double machine.

Westbrook defends during a 2016 game against the Houston Rockets. He averaged 1.6 steals and 0.4 blocks per game during the 2016–17 season.

The Triple-Double

The triple-double is a unique feat in basketball. It is when a player has more than single-digits—the double—in three different statistical categories—the triple—in a game. Almost always, one of those categories is points. The other two are usually assists and rebounds. Traditionally, it is often seen as the mark of a good player helping in all areas of the game: rebounding, passing teammates the ball, and, of course, scoring.

QUICK FACT

According to Basketball Reference, since 1983, there has been a 3.7 percent chance a triple-double will happen in an NBA game. That is about one every 27 games.

But a triple-double is not an easy thing to get in the NBA. In reality, some of the league's best players, such as Reggie Miller, only had one triple-double in their entire careers. Others had none!

But in the 2016–17 season, Russell Westbrook led the league in scoring for the second time in three years and had a league-record 42 triple-doubles. In fact, he *averaged* a triple-double for the season: 31.6 points, 10.7 rebounds, and 10.4 assists per game. He became just the second player in NBA history to manage the feat, joining Oscar Robertson, who did so in the 1961–62 season (30.8 points, 12.5 rebounds, and 11.4 assists).

It was a mind-blowing accomplishment that stunned even Robertson, though the NBA legend said he was hoping Westbrook would break his record. He even personally congratulated Westbrook on the accomplishment at the end of the season. "He has taken over the whole country with what he is doing, and it's really amazing. He's a great basketball player," Robertson told Sam Amick of *USA TODAY* in April 2017. "I'm happy for Russ."

Westbrook sometimes grew tired of reporters asking questions about the record after every game. It was a big focus of attention in the league,

Westbrook poses with the 2016–17 NBA Most Valuable Player Award, which he won with 69 percent of the vote. Westbrook also won the NBA Best Style Award for that season.

and some criticized him by saying he was overly worried about getting triple-doubles. Besides, he had bigger issues to deal with that season: Kevin Durant and the Golden State Warriors.

The Thunder played the Warriors four times in 2016–17, and Durant and the Warriors won all four meetings. In his first game against the Warriors on November 3, 2016, Westbrook wore a photographer's vest as part of his pregame outfit. The gesture was a clear jab at Durant, who is an avid photographer.

But Golden State had the last laugh. Westbrook and the Thunder did not get the chance to play Durant's Warriors in the playoffs. Golden State lost just one game in the entire postseason to win its second NBA title in three seasons.

Westbrook drives the ball against the Golden State Warriors on November 3, 2016. The Thunder lost the game by a score of 122–96.

Westbrook answers questions at a Nike Jordan Brand event. In 2017, Westbrook signed a 10-year extension to his Nike contract, which includes a chance to have his own clothing line.

Staying Put

In the summer of 2017, Oklahoma City made a number of efforts to keep their superstar with the Thunder for a long time. Westbrook's contract was up the next summer, and the team pushed to sign him to a long-term extension. Many wondered if Westbrook, frustrated by his lack of help on the Thunder, would not sign the contract and leave the team after the next season.

But the Thunder tried hard to keep Westbrook in town. Further, they got him some help. General Manager Sam Presti traded for All-Star forward Paul George in July 2017, and in September he traded for New York Knicks star Carmelo Anthony. Days before the Thunder's first preseason game, Westbrook agreed to a five-year, $205 million contract to stay in Oklahoma City.

"I've said it before, and I'll say it again, there is no place I would rather be than Oklahoma City," said Westbrook in a team statement. "I am so honored to have the opportunity to continue my career here with the Thunder."

Westbrook signed the extension, the largest in NBA history at the time, on Durant's birthday, September 29. And two weeks earlier he had signed a 10-year extension of his endorsement deal for Nike's Jordan Brand shoes that made him the company's highest-paid athlete. Westbrook is now settled financially and personally. He has set records and become one of the best in the league. All that is missing is an NBA title of his own.

His Own Man

Russell Westbrook is one of the most unique NBA superstars the game has ever seen. He has worked hard to build his NBA dream and has a rivalry with one of the NBA's best players ever. But there are many layers to the person that he is.

QUICK FACT

Westbrook often sends out tweets with a certain emoji in them. It is a man shrugging, which represents his "Why not?" saying.

Westbrook appreciates the great support he has received from Oklahoma City fans, and he has given back to the community in a big way. In 2012, he started his Why Not? Foundation, which focuses on education and family services. The organization has set up Russell's Reading Rooms in Oklahoma City public schools and has stocked them with thousands of books to encourage literacy. In 2013, Westbrook joined Thunder teammates in touring parts of the Oklahoma City area that had been devastated by tornadoes, even though he was on crutches. He won the NBA Cares Community Assist Award for the 2014–15 season.

Westbrook also has not forgotten the university that set him on the path to the NBA. In 2015, he gave a reported $1 million to UCLA's basketball program. It was the biggest donation that the school had ever received from a former basketball player.

In 2017, Westbrook published a book, *Russell Westbrook: Style Drivers*. That same year, *Sports Illustrated* named him the most

Westbrook opens a Russell's Reading Room at an elementary school in Oklahoma City. Westbrook's Why Not? Foundation has also opened reading rooms to promote literacy in Los Angeles.

fashionable athlete. Westbrook wears an outfit once and then gives it away to Goodwill Industries, a nonprofit organization, or to friends.

Along with all his other roles, Westbrook is a loving husband who married his college sweetheart, Nina Earl. On May 16, 2017, their first child, Noah Russell Westbrook, was born. Westbrook's social media profiles became filled with videos of him cooing lullabies and giggling through sing-a-longs.

QUICK FACT

In 2017, a college head coach jokingly offered Westbrook's infant son a college scholarship!

Just do not expect him to smile much on the court. When the ball is in play, Westbrook remains one of the most dangerous, most exciting players in the NBA.

TIMELINE

1988: Russell Westbrook III is born on November 12 in Long Beach, California.

1995: Russ starts playing basketball with his father.

2004: Khelcey Barrs, Russ's best friend, dies. Westbrook is noticed at an AAU event at UCLA.

2006: Westbrook begins the first of his two seasons at UCLA.

2008: Bruins reach their second straight NCAA Final Four. Westbrook and Kevin Love enter the NBA Draft. Westbrook is drafted fourth overall by the Seattle SuperSonics. Sonics move to Oklahoma City and are renamed the Thunder.

2010: Westbrook and Durant make their first playoff appearance.

2011: Westbrook is named to the NBA All-Star Team for the first time. Thunder lose to the Miami Heat in the NBA Finals.

2013: Westbrook injures his knee in the playoffs and then has surgery.

2015: Westbrook leads the NBA in scoring for the first time. Thunder miss the playoffs for first time since 2009.

2016: Thunder lose a 3–1 lead to the Golden State Warriors in the Western Conference Finals. Kevin Durant leaves the Thunder for Golden State.

2017: Westbrook sets the record for triple-doubles in an NBA season and wins the NBA MVP award. He signs a five-year, $205 million contract extension with the Thunder.

OTHER LIVING LEGENDS OF BASKETBALL

LeBron James (1984–) is a three-time NBA champion, a three-time Finals MVP, and the most recognizable athlete on the planet. James led teams to the NBA Finals in eight of his first 14 seasons.

Stephen Curry (1988–) has led the Golden State Warriors as they have become one of the most dominant teams in NBA history. He guided the Warriors to the best regular-season record in NBA history (73–9) in 2015–16. The two-time league MVP holds the NBA record for most three-pointers in a season.

Kevin Durant (1988–) is an NBA MVP who has led the league in scoring four times. He left Oklahoma City in 2016 to join a Warriors team that won 67 regular-season games and the NBA Finals. He was named Finals MVP.

James Harden (1989–) is a five-time NBA All-Star originally drafted by the Oklahoma City Thunder in 2009. In 2011–12, he was named the NBA Sixth Man of the Year, an award for the league's best performing player who comes off the bench. Harden also won a gold medal with Team USA at the 2012 London Olympics. The Thunder traded him to the Houston Rockets in 2012. In Houston, Harden became one of the NBA's most prolific scorers.

Klay Thompson (1990–) is one of the best three-point shooters in the game. Thompson and Stephen Curry form the Golden State Warriors' perimeter shooting tandem known as the "Splash Brothers." Thompson is a two-time NBA champion and a three-time All-Star. In 2017, he became the first player to score 60 points in less than 30 minutes of play on the court.

Draymond Green (1990–) is a lockdown defensive player for the Golden State Warriors. Green is one of the toughest players in the NBA. He has won two titles with Golden State and guards some of the toughest scorers in the NBA night in and night out.

Paul George (1990–) was a three-time All-Star for the Indiana Pacers before he was traded to the Thunder after the 2016–17 season. In Oklahoma City, he became a double scoring threat with Westbrook.

Kyrie Irving (1992–) is a tough-to-guard scoring threat, and he won an NBA title with the Cleveland Cavaliers before requesting a trade. Irving moved to the Boston Celtics in the summer of 2017.

Anthony Davis (1993–) is a power forward who was selected first overall by the New Orleans Hornets (now Pelicans) in the 2012 NBA Draft. In 2017, he set an NBA All-Star Game record by scoring 52 points and was named the game's MVP. He won an NCAA title with the University of Kentucky during his only college season (2011–12) and was named the tournament's Most Outstanding Player.

Giannis Antetokounmpo (1994–), known as the Greek Freak, is a superstar for the Milwaukee Bucks. He is known for his deft scoring touch and thunderous dunks that look impossible, even on replays.

GLOSSARY

elude To escape the grasp of.

franchise A team that is a member of a professional sports league.

free agency A period of time in sports during which a player is free to sign a contract to play with any team.

frustrate To cause someone to feel angry, discouraged, or upset.

inconsistent Not always acting or behaving in the same way.

investor Someone who uses money to earn more money, as in buying property or part of a company to make a future profit.

letter of intent An official decision to play sports at a college.

lockout A period of work stoppage in sports because players and team owners do not have a labor agreement.

maniac A person who behaves in a very wild way.

meniscus Cartilage within a joint, especially the knee.

mentality A particular way of thinking.

NBA Draft Combine A gathering of athletes to test their basketball skills before the NBA Draft.

scholarship Money given by a school or organization to a student to help pay for his or her education.

seed The ranking of a player or team in a competition.

semifinal The game before the championship game (or final) of a tournament.

skeptic Someone who questions or doubts something.

statistic A number used in sports to measure a player's value or performance.

FOR MORE INFORMATION

Books

Doeden, Matt. *Basketball Legends in the Making*. North Mankato, MN: Capstone Press, 2014.

Doeden, Matt. *Russell Westbrook*. Minneapolis, MN: Lerner Publications, 2017.

Hall, Brian. *Russell Westbrook*. Minneapolis, MN: SportsZone, 2017.

Hammer, Max. *Oklahoma City Thunder*. Mankato, MN: The Child's World, 2014.

Hammer, Max. *Superstars of the Oklahoma City Thunder*. Mankato, MN: Amicus, 2016.

Kelley, K. C. *Basketball Superstars 2016*. New York, NY: Scholastic, 2016.

LeBoutillier, Nate. *The Story of the Oklahoma City Thunder*. Mankato, MN: Creative Education, 2015.

Moussavi, Sam. *Oklahoma City Thunder*. New York, NY: AV2 by Weigl, 2017.

Omoth, Tyler. *A Superfan's Guide to Pro Basketball Teams*. North Mankato, MN: Capstone Press, 2017.

Omoth, Tyler. *Who's Who of Pro Basketball: A Guide to the Game's Greatest Players*. North Mankato, MN: Capstone Press, 2016.

Robinson, Tom. *Today's 12 Hottest NBA Superstars*. Mankato, MN: 12-Story Library, 2015.

Stewart, Mark. *The Oklahoma City Thunder*. Chicago, IL: Norwood House Press, 2015.

Whiting, Jim. *Oklahoma City Thunder*. Mankato, MN: Creative Education, 2018.

Whiting, Jim. *Russell Westbrook*. Hallandale, FL: Mitchell Lane Publishers, 2018.

Websites

Basketball Reference
https://www.basketball-reference.com/players/w/westbru01.html

Draft Express
http://www.draftexpress.com/profile/Russell-Westbrook-5062

ESPN
http://www.espn.com/nba/player/_/id/3468/russell-westbrook

National Basketball Association
http://www.nba.com/players/russell/westbrook/201566